CONTE

INTRODUCTION

HOW TO USE THIS

A SHORT GUIDE TO THE COMMANDMENTS	6
THE TEN COMMANDMENTS	7
DAYS 1 TO 4 BEGINNING THE WAY OF LOVE	9
DAYS 5 TO 10 WE LOVE BECAUSE GOD FIRST LOVED US	18
DAYS 11 TO 16 THE MORE WE KNOW GOD, THE MORE WE LOVE GOD	31
DAYS 17 TO 22 TO LOVE WITH ALL OUR HEART, SOUL, MIND AND STRENGTH	44
DAYS 23 TO 29 TO LOVE OUR NEIGHBOUR AS OURSELVES: IN KINDNESS AND LOVING SERVICE	57
DAYS 30 TO 34 TO LOVE OUR NEIGHBOUR AS OURSELVES: SEEKING JUSTICE AND CARE FOR THE ENVIRONMENT	72
DAYS 35 TO 40 TO LOVE OUR NEIGHBOUR AS OURSELVES IN SHARING FAITH AND GOOD NEWS	83
NEXT STEPS	96
FURTHER RESOURCES	98

INTRODUCTION
JESUS INVITES US INTO THE WAY OF LOVE

In three of the four gospels, Jesus is asked which commandment is the most important.

Jesus answers not with one commandment but with two: you shall love the Lord your God with all your heart and soul and mind and strength, and you shall love your neighbour as yourself.

These two commandments give a heartbeat, a rhythm and a shape to our lives. We are called into a deep relationship of love with God who has made us. We are also called to live a life of love with our neighbours: those who are like us and those who are not.

The daily readings in this booklet help us to explore this Way of Love: the meaning of the commandments for today. They will be helpful to beginners, those preparing for baptism or confirmation and also for those who want to go deeper in the Way.

However you take this *Pilgrim Journey*, make space. Allow God's word to dwell in you richly as we seek together to know Jesus better and to become more Christ-like in everything we are and everything we do.

STEVEN CROFT

HOW TO USE THIS BOOK

Pilgrim Journeys: The Commandments is ideal for anyone to use daily in Lent but can be used at any time of year. There are 40 daily reflections.

Each day offers:

- A **theme** for the day
- A suggested short Bible **reading** exploring the theme
- An invitation to **reflect**
- A suggestion of how to **pray**
- A prompt to **act**.

In each group of reflections we will explore a different theme relating to this wonderful Way of Love. These larger themes are outlined on the contents page and between each section.

At the end you will find some possible next steps for you on your discipleship journey as well as some further resources including other *Pilgrim* materials for you to explore, including three other *Pilgrim Journeys* exploring The Beatitudes, The Lord's Prayer and The Creeds.

Those preparing for baptism or confirmation may find this *Pilgrim Journey* helpful as part of their preparation for that commitment. There are short video reflections for each week and small group material available to accompany the reflections at **www.oxford.anglican.org/come-and-see**

A SHORT GUIDE TO THE COMMANDMENTS

The Pilgrim Way: A short guide to the Christian Faith explores what it means to share and live out our faith and identity as followers of Jesus Christ. It is shaped around four core Christian texts, including Jesus's summary of the law. This extract from *The Pilgrim Way* summarizes why these words of Jesus have been so important to the life of Christians down the ages. You might like to read this before you embark on the daily reflections, and perhaps re-visit it each week, or even try learning it by heart.

Pilgrim, how does God speak to us and teach us his ways? God teaches his people through the Bible, and above all through his Son Jesus Christ.

What is the Bible? The Bible is the library of books written over many centuries telling of God's dealings with the world. The Old Testament tells the story of God's people Israel. The New Testament tells of the good news of God's Son Jesus Christ, the gift of the Holy Spirit and the birth of the Church.

How can we trust the Bible? The Church believes that the Bible is the word of God. The Holy Spirit inspired those who wrote the Bible and enables the Church to understand God's word and to proclaim the faith afresh in each generation.

What commandments did God give Israel?
God gave Moses these commandments:

THE TEN COMMANDMENTS

I am the Lord your God:
you shall have no other gods but me.

You shall not make for yourself any idol.

You shall not dishonour
the name of the Lord your God.

Remember the Sabbath
and keep it holy.

Honour your father and mother.

You shall not commit murder.

You shall not commit adultery.

You shall not steal.

You shall not be a false witness.

You shall not covet anything
which belongs to your neighbour.

What do we learn from these commandments about God? We learn that there is only one God, and it is wrong to make gods of other things.

What do we learn from these commandments about ourselves and others? We learn that there is a rhythm and balance to life and that it is holy. We learn that the household of the family is precious, that there are things we should not do because they harm our relationship with God and one another.

How did Jesus Christ summarize the commandments? Jesus Christ says that we should love the Lord our God with all our heart, with all our soul, with all our mind, and with all our strength; and that we should love our neighbour as ourselves.

Pilgrim, how will this shape the journey of your life? I will faithfully read the Scriptures because they are a lamp to my feet and a light to my path. By God's grace, I will fashion my life according to the way of Jesus Christ.

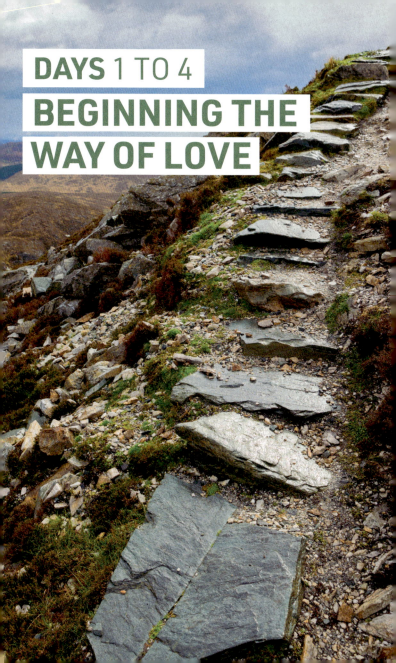

DAY 1
WHICH COMMANDMENT IS THE FIRST OF ALL?

READ Mark 12.28-34

'this is much more important than all whole burnt-offerings and sacrifices.'

REFLECT

Throughout Church history, Christians have learned about the faith through four key texts: the Apostles' Creed, the Lord's Prayer, the Beatitudes and the Commandments. People would learn them by heart and study them, especially in Lent to go deeper or to learn about faith for the first time. Sometimes they are inscribed on wooden boards in church buildings.

But which commandments? According to traditional Jewish scholars, there are 613 commandments in the Torah (the first five books in the Old Testament). Of these 248 are positive and 365 are negative. According to Exodus and Deuteronomy, God gave ten commandments to Moses, inscribed on tablets of stone. But which is the most important?

Mark, Matthew and Luke all tell the story of the two greatest commandments: to love God and love our neighbour. Notice how the question in each case is different. In Mark, a scribe asks, 'Which commandment is the first of all?' Jesus interprets the whole law as a call to the Way of Love. Love of God (Deuteronomy 6.4) and love of neighbour (Leviticus 19.18) are more important than any sacrifice.

PRAY

Take time to be still and remember God's presence. Ask the scribe's question for yourself: which is the greatest commandment? Listen for the answer.

ACT

How will you set aside time and space for reflection in the coming weeks?

DAY 2
WHAT IS THE GREATEST COMMANDMENT?

READ Matthew 22.34–40

'On these two commandments hang all the law and the prophets.'

REFLECT

Matthew's story is more combative. A member of the strict sect of the Pharisees is sent to test Jesus. There is a sense here that he is on trial. How does this healer from Galilee interpret God's holy and sacred law to which scholars devote their whole lives?

Jesus' answer is clear: through love. It is the purpose, end and meaning of our lives. We are made to love our maker with all of our heart, soul, mind and (in Mark) strength. This is the great and deep passion for which we were created, our deepest fulfilment and our joy. But there is a second, similar commandment which is equal in greatness.

We are to love our neighbours as ourselves. Love of God overflows into love for others. This love is the key which unlocks and interprets the whole of the Old Testament. On these two commandments hang all the law and the prophets (the whole of the Scriptures).

PRAY

*Blessed are those whose way is pure,
who walk in the law of the Lord.
Blessed are those who keep his testimonies
and seek him with their whole heart.*
Psalm 119.1–2

ACT

Reflect on what is at the centre of your life: where your priorities lie.

DAY 3
WHAT MUST I DO TO INHERIT ETERNAL LIFE?

READ Luke 10.25–29

'And who is my neighbour?'

REFLECT

In Mark, Jesus values the Way of Love above temple sacrifice and worship. In Matthew, Jesus says that love is the key to understanding God's written word. In Luke the emphasis is on daily life.

The lawyer is again testing Jesus but finds himself tested in return. It is the lawyer here who repeats back to us the two greatest commandments (perhaps he has been listening to Jesus for some time). These two commandments are indeed the way to life, both here and for eternity.

But the lawyer has a second question: who is my neighbour? Jesus' answer is the parable of the Good Samaritan which we will read in the coming days. But notice how Jesus' story broadens and deepens the whole meaning of the commandment. My neighbour is no longer only the person next door or the one who is like me. The second commandment is as universal and demanding and life-giving as the first.

PRAY

Lord, you have taught us that all our doings without love are nothing worth: send your Holy Spirit and pour into our hearts that most excellent gift of love.
Collect for the Second Sunday after Trinity

ACT

Who needs you to be a neighbour today?

DAY 4
THE TEN COMMANDMENTS

READ Exodus 20.1–17

'Then God spoke all these words…'

REFLECT

As Christians we come to the Ten Commandments given by Moses through Jesus' gift of the Way of Love. Love of God and neighbour is the key to understanding the law and the prophets. This love is worth more than any temple sacrifice. This love is the way of eternal life.

The Ten Commandments are given by God to Israel as part of their path to freedom, after the crossing of the Red Sea and before they enter the wilderness. The commandments follow the 'shape' of Jesus' summary.

The first tablet of the law is broadly concerned with love of God: putting God first, not misusing God's name, not making idols and setting aside time for growing this relationship of love. The second tablet of the law is concerned with love of neighbour: honouring parents, protecting the sanctity of marriage, refraining from murder and theft and conquering jealousy and greed. We will explore each commandment in more depth as we journey through Lent together. But read them today through the lens of Jesus' Way of Love.

PRAY

Christ our wisdom,
give us delight in your law,
that we may bear fruits
of patience and peace
in the kingdom of the righteous;
for your mercy's sake.
Common Worship Psalm Prayer for Psalm 1

ACT

Begin to learn the Ten Commandments by heart.

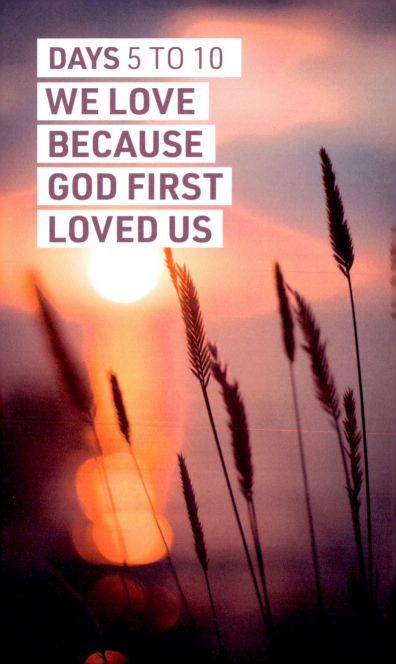

DAY 5
FOR HIS LOVE ENDURES FOR EVER

READ Psalm 136
*'Give thanks to the Lord,
for he is gracious…'*

REFLECT

'In this is love,' writes John, 'not that we loved God but that he loved us and sent his Son to be the atoning sacrifice for our sins' (1 John 4.10).

The place to begin in understanding the Way of Love is not with our feeble love of God and neighbour but with God's strong and deep and faithful love for us. Psalm 136 takes us on a journey of exploration. A powerful chorus runs through each verse of the psalm: 'for his steadfast love endures for ever'.

It's difficult to find a single word in English to capture the full meaning of the Hebrew word *hesed* here. The word 'love' alone means too many things in English. 'Steadfast love' is a good translation: this is love and regard which endures whatever the circumstances. The word has notes of strength and faithfulness and also mercy and forgiveness. This is the love God has for us which is evident in creation and the story of salvation and which takes a lifetime to explore.

PRAY

Remember us, O God,
and shape our history,
form our inward eyes
to see the shadow of the life-giving cross
in the turbulence of our time;
for his sake who died for all,
Christ our Lord.
Common Worship Psalm Prayer for Psalm 136

ACT

Set a reminder on your phone and recall the refrain from Psalm 136 hourly through the day.

DAY 6
WHEN ISRAEL WAS A CHILD, I LOVED HIM

READ Hosea 11.1–9

'I led them with cords of human kindness, with bands of love.'

REFLECT

God's call to humanity begins and ends in love. That love does not depend on our merits or actions. We cannot earn it. We do not deserve it. We are not called to know God because we are special. We are called to know God because God loves us.

Hosea preaches to a nation turning away from the God who loves them and from ways of love. Through the prophet, God calls the nation back to its very beginnings – the Exodus and the desert wanderings: 'I led them with cords of human kindness, with bands of love. I was to them like those who lift infants to their cheeks. I bent down to them and fed them.'

Even though Israel turns away, God cannot reject them or stop loving them. Hosea takes us into the heart and sorrow of God when love is not returned: 'My heart recoils within me; my compassion grows warm and tender.'

God's love for us is deep and personal. It never grows old, wears out or cuts us off. God longs to draw us home.

PRAY

O Lord! thou knowest how busy
I must be this day: if I forget thee,
do not thou forget me.
Jacob Astley (1642)

ACT

What can you build into the routine of each day to help you remember God's constant and faithful love?

DAY 7
WHO WILL SEPARATE US FROM THE LOVE OF CHRIST?

READ Romans 8.31–39

'If God is for us, who is against us?'

. . . .

REFLECT

What are the times when you have felt furthest from God? Sometimes our relationship grows distant over time for no apparent reason. Sometimes we doubt God's love because of pain or difficulty. Sometimes we cut ourselves off because of our own shortcomings.

Like Hosea, Paul reminds us that nothing can ever separate us from God's love. It is deeper and longer lasting than the entire universe. This is demonstrated in the long story of Israel's salvation and most of all in the death and resurrection of Jesus Christ and all that this death and resurrection means.

'He who did not withhold his own Son but gave him up for all of us, will he not with him also give us everything else?' (verse 32).

This is the glorious, liberating, life-changing message of the gospel. You are beloved, grounded in God's love which never changes or wavers. This is our identity and security. We are loved.

PRAY

O God, you know us to be set in the midst of so many and great dangers…
grant to us such strength and protection as may support us in all dangers and carry us through all temptations.
Collect for the Fourth Sunday before Lent

ACT

Make a note in your journal of the times you have felt most secure in the love of God.

DAY 8
GOD IS LOVE

READ 1 John 4.7–19

'Beloved, since God loved us so much, we also ought to love one another.'

REFLECT

1 John rehearses again the profound truths at the heart of the universe. God sent his Son out of love for the world. God is made known in our love for one another. Then finally and simply John focuses our minds in these three profound words: God is love.

Say them slowly and deeply in the rhythm of your breathing. God is love and those who abide in love abide in God and God abides in them. Love seeks relationship. It seeks to be returned. God's love for us invites a response of love in return. The first of the great commandments calls us to love with all our heart and soul and mind and strength – with every part of who we are. That is the way we have been loved and called into being.

Knowing that we are loved gives us courage and assurance. We stand before God and others not because of our own goodness (for we often fall short) but because of God's grace and love working in us.

PRAY

I love you, O Lord my strength.
The Lord is my crag, my fortress
and my deliverer.
Psalm 18.1

ACT

Write a short prayer of thanksgiving, rejoicing in God's love for you.

DAY 9
YOU ARE MY SON, THE BELOVED

READ Mark 1.9–15

'And just as he was coming up out of the water, he saw the heavens torn apart and the Spirit descending like a dove on him.'

REFLECT

At the beginning of his ministry Jesus comes to the River Jordan to be baptised by John. Mark strips the story back to the essentials. Jesus' baptism is the foundation and the starting point of his remarkable ministry.

In the beginning is the gift of the Spirit, descending in bodily form like a dove. And in the beginning is love. A voice comes from heaven, 'You are my Son, the Beloved; with you I am well pleased.'

The wellspring of Jesus' ministry is not a task but a relationship with the Father and the Holy Spirit: the Trinity in love. This love undergirds all that Christ will begin to do in calling new disciples, in preaching and in healing.

These words from Jesus' baptism find an echo in every service of confirmation. The Bishop addresses each candidate by name, and before the laying on of hands says, 'God has called you by name and made you his own.' We find the heart of our identity in love.

PRAY

Loving God, you have called me by name and made me your own. Thank you for the gift of life today.

ACT

Think of your favourite hymn or song which speaks of God's love. Sing or hum it as you go through the day.

DAY 10
FOR GOD SO LOVED THE WORLD

READ John 3.1–17

'Very truly I tell you, no one can see the kingdom of God without being born from above.'

....

REFLECT

John 3.16 may be the most quoted verse in the whole Bible. God loves each of us personally and deeply. But this verse goes further still. God's love is not reserved for certain people (such as you and me and people like us). God loves the entire world.

The Greek word here is *cosmos*. It means the whole universe, not just the world of people but nature, oceans, vast reaches of interstellar space, galaxies, microscopic organisms, rocks and stones. This whole cosmos is rooted in God's love.

God's purpose for the world is good and grounded in love. This is the motive for sending Jesus: not to condemn the world but that the whole world might be saved through him.

This is part of the mystery of being human: discovering that we are loved and that everyone and everything in the world is loved with the same passion and care. God's purpose for us and for the cosmos is for good.

PRAY

May God, who in Christ gives us a spring of water welling up to eternal life, perfect in us the image of his glory.
Thanksgiving for Holy Baptism blessing

ACT

Remember and give thanks for the day of your baptism.

DAY 11
YOU SHALL LOVE THE LORD YOUR GOD

READ Deuteronomy 6.1–9

'Bind them as a sign on your hand, fix them as an emblem on your forehead, and write them on the doorposts of your house...'

REFLECT

God is love and therefore, in the words of Augustine, we find our way to God not by navigation but by love. God calls us to more than obedience: God invites us into loving friendship. The purpose of the commandments is to draw us to that love, first of God and then of neighbour.

In the Book of Deuteronomy, the Ten Commandments are given by Moses in Chapter 5. Chapter 6 begins with the first and greatest, 'The Lord is our God, the Lord alone.' Note the word 'our' which again stresses relationship.

'You shall love the Lord your God with all your heart, and with all your soul, and with all your might.' Keeping the commandments is the first step in loving God with our heart and soul and might. In a similar way, the love we have for God provides the right way to temper and interpret the commandments and ensure that they give life generation after generation.

PRAY

Most merciful redeemer,
grant that we may know you more clearly,
love you more dearly,
and follow you more nearly,
day by day.
after Richard of Chichester (1253)

ACT

Write the commandments out and put them in a symbolic and prominent place.

DAY 12
THE LORD IS MY SHEPHERD

READ Psalm 23

'Surely goodness and loving mercy shall follow me all the days of my life...'

REFLECT

One of the ways we demonstrate our love for God is in prayer and worship. Psalm 23 offers us profound and beautiful words of love which we say back to the God who loves us. The psalm turns around the two beautiful images of shepherd and host.

The first part of the psalm unfolds God's constant love in all the movement of a life: the imagery of rest and still waters when we are stressed, of guidance when we are lost and deep comfort in times of sorrow. The second part celebrates God's welcome to his own table, to offer strength and joy and to abide and to be at home with the Lord both in this life and the life to come.

No matter how many times we offer the psalm in prayer there are always different moments of resonance as we sing out our love and sing of God's constant care for us.

PRAY

Pray the words of Psalm 23 slowly and deliberately, pondering each line.

ACT

Reflect on what Psalm 23 will mean for your future.

DAY 13
ANY CONSOLATION FROM LOVE

READ Philippians 2.1–11

'having the same love, being in full accord and of one mind.'

REFLECT

'The consolation from love' is a beautiful phrase. It captures the comfort and encouragement of a friend, a light in darkness, water in the desert and hope in a time of despair.

The Philippians are struggling as we do with the ordinary gritty experience of church life and fracture. Paul directs them again to the bigger picture, to the whole story of salvation and therefore to the story of God's love. Paul points them to Christ and especially the humility of Christ who emptied himself and took the form of a slave.

This incarnation of love leads to Christ's offering of his life on the cross for love. And this offering of himself leads in turn to resurrection: to God lifting Christ up and setting Jesus at the centre and pinnacle of creation.

This beautiful panorama draws our eyes away from ourselves and our momentary troubles and fixes them again and again on the lover's beauty and perfection.

PRAY

*Almighty God, whose most dear Son went
not up to joy but first he suffered pain,
and entered not into glory
before he was crucified:
mercifully grant that we,
walking in the way of the cross
may find it none other than
the way of life and peace.*
Collect for the Third Sunday of Lent

ACT

What can you do today to preserve and mend the unity of Christ's church?

DAY 14
MY BELOVED IS MINE AND I AM HIS

READ Song of Solomon 2.8–17

'Arise, my love, my fair one, and come away.'

REFLECT

We are to love God with all our heart and soul and mind and strength. The more clearly we see God the more we are drawn into adoration and devotion.

The Song of Songs is a series of love poems, celebrating human and physical love and affection. But Christians have long interpreted these words as expressing also the power of God's love to move and stir our souls with longing.

Sometimes God's love calls us further up and farther in. Sometimes that same love will call us to rest and simply to be in God for a time. Sometimes God's love awakens us as the spring awakens the cold earth after a deep winter. Sometimes we are stirred to deep devotion and emotion in poetry or song or contemplation.

God's love is not one way to be but deep and endless and full of variety: now joyous, now solemn, now strong, now playful, never ending and always new.

PRAY

Lord, you know I that I love you.
Lord, you know that I love you.
Lord, you know everything;
you know that I love you.
from John 21.15−18

ACT

What do you believe God is calling you to do? Who should you discuss this with?

DAY 15
FROM ONE DEGREE OF GLORY TO ANOTHER

READ 2 Corinthians 3.12-18

'Since, then, we have such a hope, we act with great boldness...'

REFLECT

Paul recognises that the contemplation of love has the power to change and transform the one who loves. When we spend time with God, we grow (ever so slowly) more alive and at the same time we grow into the family likeness.

Paul uses here the example of Moses who would enter into God's presence without a veil, in order to speak with God face to face (Exodus 34.29-35). Moses' face shone after these meetings, so much so that he needed to wear a veil in order to mix again with the congregation outside his meeting place with God.

Like Moses, we all have the invitation to speak with God face to face as we spend time in God's presence in worship and prayer. Like Moses too, we are called in some small way to reflect God's love and power and glory to those around as we have spent time in God's presence. The way of contemplation is the way of change.

PRAY

Merciful God,
you have prepared for those who love you
such good things as pass our understanding:
pour into our hearts such love toward you
that we, loving you in all things and above all things,
may obtain your promises,
which exceed all that we can desire;
through Jesus Christ our Lord.
Collect for the Sixth Sunday after Trinity

ACT

Who do you know who most reminds you of Jesus and brings you into the presence of God?

DAY 16
HENCE SHE HAS SHOWN GREAT LOVE

READ Luke 7.36–50

'Your faith has saved you; go in peace.'

. . . .

REFLECT

The story of the Simon the Pharisee and the woman who was forgiven captures what should be our own response of love. This woman is called a sinner, someone who was outcast from God and from people because of the choices she has made.

The woman says nothing in the passage yet her actions speak volumes. She dares to risk rejection. She bathes Jesus' (dirty) feet with her tears of sorrow and of joy, she dries them with her hair, she kisses and anoints them with the precious ointment.

But why this deep devotion? This unnamed woman can see far more clearly than Simon. She sees how much she has been forgiven, how great her debt that has been cancelled and how much she has been restored to new life.

It is because our sins have been forgiven that we too are called to show great love. This love is drawn from us as we reflect on how far God has brought us.

PRAY

Alleluia. Praise the Lord, O my soul:
while I live I will praise the Lord;
as long as I have any being,
I will sing praises to my God.
Psalm 146.1

ACT

What would be your equivalent of this woman's action of costly devotion? How will you offer this love?

DAY 17
I AM THE LORD YOUR GOD

READ Deuteronomy 5.1–15

'Hear, O Israel, the statutes and ordinances that I am addressing to you today…'

REFLECT

The Ten Commandments have a unique place in the Bible. They are the only body of law repeated twice. The Lord speaks them directly to the assembly at the crossing of the Red Sea. They are inscribed on the two stone tablets kept in the ark. They stand at the head of a whole tradition of interpretation in Jewish and Christian teaching. They have historically formed part of Christian instruction for baptism and confirmation and have an honoured place in our liturgy.

The first table of the commandments, broadly speaking, focuses on our relationship with God and the second on how we love our neighbours. The two are clearly interlinked.

The commandments are always to be read mindful of God's grace and saving acts. They are given after the crossing of the Red Sea. Christians read them in the light of the cross. They are not a way to earn God's favour but to respond to God's love. They flow from a fresh statement of God's name and God's identity: 'I am the Lord your God.'

PRAY

The law of the Lord is perfect,
reviving the soul;
the testimony of the Lord is sure
and gives wisdom to the simple.
Psalm 19.7

ACT

Are you able to learn the Ten Commandments by heart? Which do you have most difficulty remembering?

DAY 18
PRESENT YOUR BODIES AS A LIVING SACRIFICE

READ Romans 12.1–8

'Do not be conformed to this world, but be transformed by the renewing of your minds...'

REFLECT

The starting point of the commandments is 'you shall have no other gods before me.' This first commandment puts almighty God, maker of heaven and earth, above all.

For ancient Israel, fulfilling this command meant an elaborate system of sacrifice: making offerings to God from crops and herds as an expression of love and devotion and as a way of seeking God's forgiveness.

For the Christian, Jesus Christ has offered the one, perfect sacrifice for sin. In response we are called to offer our whole lives and, in Paul's vivid phrase, to become a living sacrifice. We live our whole lives for

God and devote ourselves in worship and in prayer.

Like all the commandments, properly understood, the first is a liberation. We are set free from needing to win God's favour and from serving other gods which are projections of human imagination or power. Instead we are to seek God's way, to use our best gifts in God's service and to seek God's glory in all we do.

PRAY

Through [Jesus] we offer you our souls and bodies to be a living sacrifice.
Send us out in the power of your Spirit to live and work to your praise and glory.
Prayer after Communion

ACT

What is the living sacrifice you will bring to God today?

DAY 19
THESE ARE YOUR GODS, O ISRAEL

READ Exodus 32.1–6

'Come, make gods for us, who shall go before us...'

....

REFLECT

The story of the golden calf is one of the most powerful and spectacular stories of failure in the entire Bible. The second commandment is clear. You shall not make for yourself an idol. Almighty God cannot be limited to the image of anything in creation.

But no sooner have the commandments been given than the Israelites entice Aaron to fashion a golden calf. They bow down to the calf, offer sacrifices and rise up to revel. The long battle between the worship of the living God and the worship of idols in ancient Israel has begun. It continues throughout the Old Testament.

The Israelites are foolish and proud and deceived here. Yet so are we whenever we make idols in our own lives and bow down to worship the gods of money, fame, power or technology. The first two commandments are two sides of the same coin. To love God with all our heart, soul, mind and strength is to have no other gods and to turn away for ever from the making of idols.

PRAY

Were the whole realm of nature mine,
that were a present far too small.
Love so amazing, so divine,
demands my soul, my life, my all.
Isaac Watts (1707)

ACT

Examine your own life: what idols are you in danger of making?

DAY 20
TAMING THE TONGUE

READ James 3.1–12

'How great a forest is set ablaze by a small fire! And the tongue is a fire.'

REFLECT

Whenever I teach small groups about the commandments, I begin by asking people how many they can name without looking. Often they will get to seven or eight. The third commandment is almost always forgotten: 'You shall not make wrongful use of the name of the Lord your God…'.

This commandment follows on from the first two: God's name is precious and captures something of

God's nature. To love God means to honour that name. The third commandment is preserved in the first line of the Lord's Prayer: 'hallowed be' God's name.

Swearing is, in essence, making wrongful use of the name of the Lord our God. Swearing and foul speech offer a window on our souls. One of the ways in which Christians are called to be distinctive is to try daily to control our tongues and what we say, so that everything is to the glory of God. As the letter of James tells us, this can seem almost impossible at times – yet this too is part of loving God and neighbour.

PRAY

Make me a clean heart, O God,
and renew a right spirit within me.
Psalm 51.11

ACT

What do you need to set right in your own patterns of speech? Make a note of your resolutions.

DAY 21
THE SABBATH WAS MADE FOR HUMANKIND

READ Mark 2.23–27

'Look, why are they doing what is not lawful on the sabbath?'

REFLECT

The final command in this first table is, 'Observe the sabbath day and keep it holy...'. Exodus 20 refers back to God creating the sabbath in Genesis 2.1. Deuteronomy 5 refers to liberation from the land of Egypt. Life should not be all work for anyone. Yet, unless checked, work has a disturbing habit of taking over everything and turning us back into slaves.

In Jesus' day, the sabbath itself had been turned into a burden by some who placed new restrictions on God's people. Jesus is clear: this commandment (and by implication the others) are primarily given for the blessing and benefit of humankind. They are not intended to surround us with arbitrary and burdensome restrictions and the opportunity to judge one another.

Sabbath is interpreted in many different ways today. It is a vital and wonderful gift offering time for rest and a reset, recreation and joy. Without space and time for repair, our lives become more and more stretched and thin. Abundant life means time for abundant rest.

PRAY

*The Lord is my shepherd;
therefore can I lack nothing.
He makes me lie down in green pastures
and leads me beside still waters.
He shall refresh my soul...*
Psalm 23.1–3

ACT

Review your patterns of weekly rest and sabbath. What do you need to change?

DAY 22
A QUIET SOUL

READ Psalm 131

'O Lord, my heart is not proud; my eyes are not raised in haughty looks.'

....

REFLECT

The first table of the Ten Commandments offers us four different ways to be drawn deeper into loving God with all our heart, soul, mind and strength. The first is to dwell on who God is, wondering at his nature and the story of salvation ('I am the Lord your God…').

The second is to ensure that God alone is our first love and to turn away from any idols we have made. The third is to do all we can to ensure that everything we say and do is honouring to God. The fourth is to make time and space each week for worship and rest, to honour God in the rhythm of our lives.

Psalm 131 offers us a profound picture of human contentment and rest and of the soul with God: a weaned child in its mother's arms, perfectly at peace. This is our resting place at the beginning and end of each day, a place of trust, forgiveness, strength and joy. This too is what it means to love the Lord our God with all our heart and soul and mind and strength.

PRAY

Eternal God, calm and quieten our souls; keep us humble and full of wonder and trusting as we live in your love.
Common Worship Psalm Prayer for Psalm 131

ACT

Take time out of your day today, in the midst of all you are doing, to rest in the love of God for you.

DAYS 23 TO 29
TO LOVE OUR NEIGHBOUR AS OURSELVES: IN KINDNESS AND LOVING SERVICE

DAY 23
AS THE LORD YOUR GOD COMMANDED YOU

READ Deuteronomy 5.16–21

'so that your days may be long and that it may go well with you...'

REFLECT

The second table of the Ten Commandments turns from love of God to love of neighbour. It lays down God's key expectations for human relationships: honour and respect between the generations; turning away from violence and hatred; faithfulness in marriage; respecting the property of others; speaking and seeking truth; and watching over our own desires and greed.

These six commandments are deceptively simple. But the more we look, the more we see the interrelationships and the complexity. One is positive, five are negative ('You shall not…') but each has both a positive and a negative aspect. Only one has a promise attached but in Scripture it is possible to discover and set promises besides each one.

These commandments too stand as the source and spring of a deep ethical tradition of how men and women relate to one another and live together well. That tradition is continually refined and adapted in different contexts yet these commandments stand still as a summary of what it means to love well.

PRAY

The statutes of the Lord are right and rejoice the heart; the commandment of the Lord is pure and gives light to the eyes.
Psalm 19.8

ACT

Look ahead to the coming week. Can you anticipate events and encounters which will cause you to remember each of these commandments?

DAY 24
YOUR GOD, MY GOD
READ Ruth 1.1–18

'Where you go, I will go; where you lodge, I will lodge…'

....

REFLECT

'Honour your father and your mother,' says the commandment, setting honour and respect for older generations and within families as a benchmark of love for all time. Yet every culture recognises that patterns of family life are seldom neat and never perfect. So the principles behind the commandment become a living law to be applied differently in different circumstances.

KINDNESS AND LOVING SERVICE

Ruth's vow to Naomi is one of the most significant moments in the story of the Old Testament, leading to the birth of David and ultimately to the birth of Jesus (Matthew 1.5). Ruth applies the principle behind the sixth commandment to her relationship with Naomi, her mother-in-law. In return, Ruth finds her own honoured place among the people of God. Two women related only by marriage form their own household and together forge a vital link in the story of God's salvation.

Ruth's story reminds us that families cross generations and come in all shapes and sizes. We are bound together by love and respect, one generation for another. That love and respect brings stability for society and protection for individuals against loneliness, one of the great diseases of our age.

PRAY

Give thanks today for those who are part of your immediate family and community.

ACT

Renew your commitment to your family group and review the respect and honour you give.

DAY 25
YOU HAVE HEARD THAT IT WAS SAID

READ Matthew 5.17–30

'Do not think that I have come to abolish the law or the prophets...'

REFLECT

On face value the command to do no murder is very simple. The outlawing of murder stands at the heart of most penal codes the world over. Deuteronomy will go on to distinguish manslaughter and accidental death from murder and provide guidance on how to test difficult cases. The debates around murder and the taking of human life have historically played a part in the great ethical debates around pacifism and war (where the majority tradition has been that taking up arms in a just war is right) and now in the debate around euthanasia and the right to life.

Jesus, too, stands at the heart of the interpretation of this and other commandments. In some places, Jesus steers us towards a more humane and merciful interpretation of the law (for example on the sabbath or the punishment for adultery). In others, as here, Jesus takes us deeper still and connects outward acts with inner motives: murder with jealousy and adultery with lust. The common direction is to turn towards the principles of love at the heart of the law.

PRAY

Keep us, good Lord, under the shadow of your mercy and, as you have bound us to yourself in love, leave us not who call upon your name, but grant us your salvation, made known in the cross of Jesus Christ our Lord.
Common Worship Psalm Prayer for Psalm 91

ACT

Examine yourself. Are you nursing hatred? Is there anyone you need to forgive?

DAY 26
YOUR BODY IS A TEMPLE OF THE HOLY SPIRIT

READ Corinthians 6.12–20

'The body is meant not for fornication but for the Lord, and the Lord for the body.'

REFLECT

Paul too interprets and reinterprets the commandments for his own generation and for the Church in every age. The seventh commandment, to not commit adultery, is primarily around faithfulness within marriage, the cornerstone of stability, the family unit and the bringing up of children in stable households.

Jesus models forgiveness even for those caught in the act of adultery yet also underlines the sanctity of marriage. Paul extends this debate into sexual promiscuity generally: our Christian faith and call to holiness affect the whole of our lives including our bodies and sexuality. Today this impacts the conversations around human sexuality where many Christians believe that a new scientific understanding of human attraction should lead to the blessing of same-sex relationships while others seek to uphold a traditional view of marriage between a man and a woman.

Yet all sides of the debate on this issue agree that sex is an important part of life and conversations about how we live well as Christians must include how we glorify God with our bodies.

PRAY

Search me out, O God, and know my heart; try me and examine my thoughts.
See if there is any way of wickedness in me and lead me in the way everlasting.
Psalm 139.23–24

ACT

Review whether there are areas of your life where you need pastoral support or forgiveness.

DAY 27
IF I HAVE DEFRAUDED ANYONE OF ANYTHING

READ Luke 19.1–10

'Today salvation has come to this house...'

REFLECT

Stealing is a serious matter and Zacchaeus is a thief. His job is to collect taxes on behalf of the hated Roman occupiers. It was an accepted practice to collect more than was strictly due and for the tax collectors to line their pockets from the proceeds.

An outcast in Jericho's polite society, Zacchaeus is hated, not loved, by his neighbours. Yet Jesus seeks to heal this rift. Zacchaeus breaks the eighth commandment for a living, as it were. He hides up a tree wanting to see but not to be seen. It is a remarkable thing that Jesus singles him out in order to stay at his house.

The effect on this lifelong 'sinner' is remarkable. Zacchaeus reverses his theft by giving half his wealth away instantly and promising to pay back anyone he has robbed four times as much.

Regularly breaking the commandments shapes and hardens character – but God's grace yet breaks in and brings change.

PRAY

Take my silver and my gold;
Not a mite would I withhold;
Take my intellect, and use
Every power as Thou shalt choose.
Frances Ridley Havergal (1874)

ACT

Would this be a good day to give some money to a charity as an act of thanksgiving to God?

DAY 28
AND SPEAK THE TRUTH FROM THEIR HEART

READ Psalm 15

'Lord who may dwell in your tabernacle? Who may rest upon your holy hill?'

REFLECT

God's people are to be people of truth. The command to not bear false witness against your neighbour covers the whole area of truth and integrity before God and before others.

The Psalms together are based on the values of the Ten Commandments. Psalm 15 is a list in verse of the key qualities of those who would abide with God. Many of the qualities in the list are to do with the consistency of what we say: speaking truth, not slandering with the tongue, not taking up a reproach against neighbours, and standing by oaths and promises.

Integrity is a rare quality in public life and often in the Church. Exaggeration, gossip and lies can be seductive. We love image more than truth sometimes. But our calling is to witness to the one who is the truth and this too is part of loving our neighbours as ourselves.

PRAY

Lord, lead us to our heavenly home by single steps of self-restraint and deeds of righteousness; through the grace of Jesus Christ our Lord.
Common Worship Psalm Prayer for Psalm 15

ACT

Examine your use of social media. How much do you pay attention to truth in what you are consuming and what you are giving out?

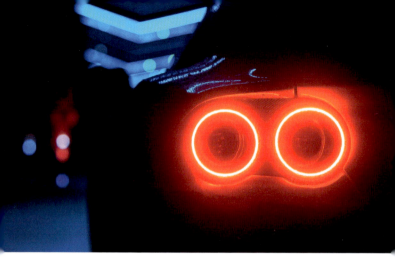

DAY 29
DISORDERED DESIRE

READ Samuel 11.1–13

'he saw from the roof a woman bathing; the woman was very beautiful.'

....

REFLECT

The tenth commandment is different from all the others. 'You shall not covet' takes us from the realm of speech and action to the right ordering of our desires. There is a profound understanding that sin begins deep within, from our inner motivation. This also needs to be right before God.

KINDNESS AND LOVING SERVICE

This is a far-reaching insight and the final commandment is much more open ended. It covers sexual desire, houses, fields and animals, ending with 'anything that belongs to your neighbour'.

David's sin in 2 Samuel begins with disordered desire. He abuses his power and status first to sleep with Bathsheba, then to attempt to cover his transgression, then to have Uriah killed in battle. Sin compounds rapidly. God's judgement is all too real. The story begins the succession narrative of trouble after trouble on David's house, all flowing from disordered desires. Part of our continued growth as Christians is to watch over where our hearts are leading us.

PRAY

Reflect on these words of Jesus from the Sermon on the Mount: 'If your right eye causes you to sin, tear it out...'.

ACT

Examine your inner eye and your desires. Where might you need to acknowledge coveting what belongs to your neighbour?

DAY 30
OUR FIRST COMMISSION
READ Genesis 2.15–25

'to till and keep the earth…'

REFLECT

The world is facing a climate catastrophe and an environmental emergency. Public awareness of the danger the planet faces grows year by year with extreme weather events, nature degradation and a terrible increase in war and economic migration, much of which is climate related.

One of the principal causes of climate change is greed: wanting more and more for ourselves and our generation and not matching our desires to what is sustainable for the earth. Our entire economic system is geared to wanting and consuming more and more. The entire advertising industry feeds our greed.

According to Genesis, humanity's first commission is to till (literally to serve) the earth: to ensure its rich biodiversity and sustainability for future generations. We have failed and must urgently now address the consequences of our covetousness. This means an honest and open conversation about what is enough for life as a vital part of what it means to love our neighbour as ourselves.

PRAY

Creator of our common home,
You fill the earth and sea and sky with life.
Forgive us our neglect of your creation
The choking waste of our pollution
The damage done by careless habits
And our indifference to future generations.

ACT

What is the next step on your personal journey to care for the earth? What is the next step on the journey for your local church?

DAY 31
AND WHO IS MY NEIGHBOUR?
READ Luke 10.29–37
'Go and do likewise.'

REFLECT

The lawyer in Luke's story of the two commandments presses Jesus further with the question, 'And who is my neighbour?' Is it the people who live next door? Is it the people I know? Is it those who are just like me?

Jesus' answer in the parable of the Good Samaritan is powerful and shocking for every generation. Who was a neighbour to the man who fell among thieves? Neither the priest nor the Levite but the foreigner. The person of a different race and religion crossed the road, crossed boundaries and cancelled plans in order to love and support the one in need. The one who loves his neighbour is the one who shows him mercy.

Jesus' final response to the lawyer is a challenge to every reader of the gospel. This love and practical care is to shape our lives: 'Go and do likewise.'

PRAY

Oh Lord, the Son,
In a world full of anger and frustration,
Teach us, your servants, your friends,
your sisters and your brothers,
To overturn the tables
and tear down the fences
Which turn away
the hungry and homeless:
To feed and house the disciple
that knocks on our door
In the guise of the stranger,
And to find the Love
we seek in loving others.
'Love Your Neighbour' Prayer,
Diocese of St Albans

ACT

What do you need to do today to love your neighbour as yourself?

DAY 32
THE ISAIAH VISION

READ Isaiah 65.17-25

*'They shall not labour in vain,
or bear children for calamity...'*

REFLECT

Love of neighbour gives birth continually to a fresh vision for human life and flourishing. If my neighbour is the stranger then love for that neighbour needs to extend beyond acts of kindness to working for a better world.

The prophets hold out this vision and none more so than the Book of Isaiah. The Isaiah Vision is born out of the pain and failure of exile. It is a cosmic vision of a new heaven and a new earth. What it offers is both simple and deeply humane.

A good city is where children are not at risk of death, where adults live well into old age, where people build houses and live in them. So many people in so many parts of the world lack these basic necessities of human life while others have so much they do not need.

To love my neighbour means to take this vision and

this challenge seriously. For every Christian the call to justice is a part of our discipleship. For many it is a lifelong vocation.

PRAY

Give us, O God, the vision
which can see Your love in the world
in spite of human failure.
Give us the faith to trust Your goodness
in spite of our ignorance and weakness.
Give us the knowledge that we may continue to pray
with understanding hearts.
And show us what each one of us can do
to set forward the coming of the day of universal peace.
A Prayer from Apollo 8 for Universal Justice, Frank Borman (1968)

ACT

Write down your vision for your local community. What would you change? Share that vision with a friend.

DAY 33
DO JUSTICE, LOVE KINDNESS, WALK HUMBLY

READ Micah 6.6–8

'He has told you, O mortal, what is good…'

REFLECT

The tenth commandment is in some ways the mirror image of the command to love our neighbours as ourselves. Both have their roots in the ordering of desire. We are not to covet what is not ours. The root of what it means to covet is selfishness and greed: loving ourselves to the exclusion of everyone else.

To love our neighbours we need a healthy sense of who we are: it's not wrong to love ourselves in that way – for we know that God loves us and calls us. But love of neighbour turns our life inside out: we discover gradually that we have a responsibility to the whole world and to creation to work for justice.

That can at times be overwhelming – even when we remember that this is impossible without God's strength. But Micah brings us back to the simplicity beyond complexity, which is priceless.

What does the Lord require of you?

To do justice and to love kindness and to walk humbly with your God.

Christian, this is your life's work.

PRAY

O Lord, open my eyes that I may see the needs of others
Open my ears that I may hear their cries;
Open my heart so that they need not be without succor;
Let me not be afraid to defend the weak because of the anger of the strong,
Nor afraid to defend the poor because of the anger of the rich.
Show me where love and hope and faith are needed,
And use me to bring them to those places.
For Courage to Do Justice, Alan Paton

ACT

Look out for opportunities for random acts of kindness this day.

DAY 34
AND THE GREATEST OF THESE IS LOVE

READ Corinthians 13

'Love never ends.'

REFLECT

The New Testament is written in Greek, which has several words for the English word 'love'. *Eros* signifies romantic and sexual love. *Philia* describes the love between friends. *Storge* means the affection between family members. Then the fourth love is *agape* (pronounced 'agapay'). This is the word for love in most of the New Testament texts including Jesus' summary of the law and here in 1 Corinthians 13.

Agape is self-giving love to those outside the bonds of romantic love, friendship or family. It's love for the undeserving and those we do not like. This love mirrors God's steadfast covenant love for us. It doesn't change or waver.

It is this love which is the more excellent way described in 1 Corinthians 13 and which should be at the heart of the life of the Church. This is the love Jesus shows to all who come to him. It is this love we are called to embody. It is this love which will endure to eternity.

Hope will be realised when we see God face to face. Faith will not be needed when we are with God for eternity. But love for God and neighbour will endure through life eternal.

PRAY

Lord, help me to love others
as you love me,
with patience and kindness,
faithfulness and hope.

ACT

Reflect on your church or your school or your workplace. How much love is there? How can you help that love to grow?

DAYS 35 TO 40

TO LOVE OUR NEIGHBOUR AS OURSELVES IN SHARING FAITH AND GOOD NEWS

DAY 35
SHARING GOOD NEWS

READ 2 Kings 7.3–11

'What we are doing is wrong. This is a day of good news…'

REFLECT

There is one more aspect of love to explore as we reflect on the commandments. As Christians we have found life's greatest treasure: the joy of knowing Jesus, being known by him and living in his way; the assurance of sins forgiven and the promise of resurrection.

If we love those around us, we will want to gently and clearly bear witness to this treasure. Christians call this 'evangelism' – sharing good news. Another definition of evangelism is 'one beggar telling another beggar where to find bread'.

2 Kings tells the story of four leprous men outside the gates of Samaria. They discover the whole city has been saved after a long siege. The enemy has withdrawn in the night. At first they keep all the good things for themselves and stash them away. But then they come to their senses and realise they have a tremendous responsibility to share this good news. Telling others so that they can share in salvation is also our calling and part of what it means to love.

PRAY

Almighty God, who called your church to bear witness that you were in Christ reconciling the world to yourself: help us to proclaim the good news of your love, that all who hear it may be drawn to you…
Collect for the Thirteenth Sunday after Trinity

ACT

Make a short list of those God is leading you to pray for in your own work of witness.

DAY 36
OPENING HEARTS, OPENING HOMES

READ Acts 16.11–15

'The Lord opened her heart to listen eagerly...'

REFLECT

Acts tells the story of the spread of the gospel across the Roman Empire. Paul and his companions come eventually to Philippi in Greece, a Roman colony. They gather by the river where they have heard there is a place of prayer. There they meet Lydia, already a worshipper of God, already seeking.

There is a beautiful double hospitality in the way that Acts describes Lydia here. First the Lord opens her heart to listen eagerly to what was said by Paul. Then, immediately, Lydia opens her home to Paul and to the apostles and her house becomes the base for the first church on European soil.

This is the way the gospel spread in the ancient world through the power of the Holy Spirit: one person telling another and establishing new congregations in many different places. This is the way the gospel still spreads today – but the church, in love, must tell the story.

PRAY

Lord I hear your gentle call;
I open the door of my heart to you.
Come in.

ACT

Write down the story of how you came to faith and how you would tell that story to a friend.

DAY 37
KNOWING WHEN TO SPEAK

READ 1 Peter 3.13–18

'Always be ready to make your defence to anyone who demands from you an account of the hope that is in you…'

....

REFLECT

Some Christians are gifted evangelists: able to talk naturally about their faith to strangers in ways which draw others to Christ. Most of us don't have that gift. We shouldn't feel guilty or awkward about this. Nor should we press our faith on those who don't really want to know.

1 Peter describes a better and more loving way: be ready to share our faith but also wait until we are asked. That will mean some reflection and

preparation to be ready for the most natural questions: Why does your faith mean so much to you? What do you mean you were at Church yesterday? Whatever we say, the two watchwords of gentleness and respect – two aspects of love – need to run through all we say.

It may mean regular prayer for family and friends who don't yet know Christ for themselves. But it will mainly mean patience and continuing to bear witness through practical service and kindness, through using the gifts we do have in God's service and through living our lives to the full.

PRAY

Lord, grant to your servants to speak your word with all boldness, while you stretch out your hand to heal, and signs and wonders are performed through the name of your holy servant Jesus.
from Acts 4.29

ACT

Try and be watchful this week for an opportunity to bear witness to God's love.

DAY 38
THE NEW COMMANDMENT

READ John 13.31–38
'By this everyone will know that you are my disciples…'

REFLECT

The day before Good Friday is Maundy Thursday. The word 'maundy' comes from the Latin word *mandatum* which means 'commandment'. This is the day we remember the gift of Holy Communion as Jesus celebrates the last supper with his friends. This is the day we remember the foot-washing and Jesus' practical love and service to his friends. And this is the day when we remember the new commandment for the disciples.

We are to love the Lord our God with all our

heart, soul, mind and strength. We are to love our neighbour as ourselves. But the Church is characterised by another love also. We are called to love one another as Christ has loved us: to be bound together in ties of love and affection and respect and sacrifice.

This love is seldom easy. Christians are not always easy to love. But Jesus gives this new commandment a special place in the witness we bear to the world: 'By this everyone will know that you are my disciples, if you have love for one another.'

· ·

PRAY

Loving Lord Jesus,
Thank you for your great love for me and for all your Church.
Help me to love my sisters and brothers
Especially ……………… and ……………… this day
And so bear witness to your world.

· ·

ACT

Is there someone in the church you find it especially hard to love? Are you able to imagine and then carry out an act of kindness for them?

DAY 39
IT IS FINISHED
READ John 19.16–30

'There they crucified him...'

REFLECT

In his first letter, John writes 'We love because he first loved us' (1 John 4.19). Here on Good Friday we see that love's extent and depth. Jesus offers his life for the sins of the whole world – and for our own sins.

Jesus gives his life on the cross: his life is not taken from him. Jesus' most telling words on the cross are, 'It is finished.' The crucifixion is not an accidental ending to a wonderful life or a fruitful ministry cut short by tragedy. The crucifixion is the reason the Son of God took flesh: to give his life for the sins of the world. The good shepherd lays down his life for the sheep.

This is why Jesus is able to see his life's work completed on a lonely hillside outside Jerusalem, watched only by his mother and a few close friends. This is love's supreme gift, the assurance of our own worth and of Christ's gift to us.

In the words of the hymn which will be sung all over the world today: 'Love so amazing, so divine, demands my soul, life, my all.'

PRAY

When I survey the wond'rous Cross
On which the Prince of Glory dy'd,
My richest Gain I count but Loss,
And pour Contempt on all my Pride.
Isaac Watts (1707)

ACT

Spend some time in your imagination before the cross of Christ. What do you learn?

DAY 40
FINAL WORDS

READ John 21.15–25

'Lord, you know that I love you.'

REFLECT

Simon Peter's conversation with the risen Jesus on the seashore is many things: a restoration after Peter's threefold denial, a healing, a commission.

But at the end of this journey, notice most of all that this is a conversation about love from beginning to end. In love, Jesus takes his hurting disciple aside. Love is the centre of his question 'do you love me more than these?'

Peter no longer makes extravagant claims of devotion but replies from a humble and honest heart: 'Lord, you know that I love you.' Then comes the commission which is also expressed in the language of love and the image of the good shepherd: feed my lambs, tend my sheep, feed my sheep.

For Simon Peter and for us, love's journey will continue after the resurrection into new callings and new ventures. But at the centre of our Christian life will be our calling to love the Lord our God with all our heart, soul, mind and strength and to love our neighbour as ourselves. Thank you for your fellowship on this journey.

PRAY

Lord, you know that I love you.
Lord, you know that I love you.
Lord, you know that I love you.

ACT

Look back over these 40 days of readings. What have you learned? What will you take with you?

NEXT STEPS

A COURSE FOR THE CHRISTIAN JOURNEY

JOIN A LOCAL GROUP USING THE 'PILGRIM' COURSE

Pilgrim: A Course for the Christian Journey is widely used across and beyond the Church of England. *Pilgrim* offers eight short courses designed to be used by small groups of people who are exploring the Christian faith. The course is based around four core texts, including The Creeds. Find out more about *Pilgrim* books, eBooks, DVDs and online resources via **www.pilgrimcourse.org**

EXPLORE OTHER *PILGRIM JOURNEY* BOOKLETS

Other booklets in this series include **Pilgrim Journeys: The Lord's Prayer**, **Pilgrim Journeys: The Beatitudes** and **Pilgrim Journeys: The Creeds**.

JOIN IN WITH FURTHER DISCIPLESHIP CAMPAIGNS

Visit **www.churchofengland.org** to sign up to take part in future discipleship initiatives from the Church of England. It is free to sign up and you can easily opt out at any time.

TAKE PART IN *THY KINGDOM COME*

Thy Kingdom Come is a global prayer movement that invites Christians around the world to pray for more people to come to know Jesus. What started in 2016 as an invitation from the Archbishops of Canterbury and York to the Church of England has grown into an international and ecumenical call to prayer.

During the 11 days of *Thy Kingdom Come* – between Ascension and Pentecost – it is hoped that everyone who participates will deepen their friendship with Jesus, bring others to know Jesus or know him better, and come to know that every aspect of their life is the stuff of prayer.

For more details and a wide range of resources visit **www.thykingdomcome.global**

FURTHER RESOURCES

Stephen Cottrell, Steven Croft, Paula Gooder, Robert Atwell, *Pilgrim Book 3: The Commandments*, Church House Publishing.

This 6-session course would be ideal for a group to use during Lent (or at any time) alongside the material for individuals in this book.

Available from www.chpublishing.co.uk

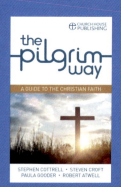

Stephen Cottrell, Steven Croft, Paula Gooder, Robert Atwell, *The Pilgrim Way: A short guide to the Christian faith*, Church House Publishing.

The Church of England website also allows you to explore a digital version with video, images and further resources exploring the Christian faith and what difference it makes to a wide range of Christians: **www.churchofengland.org/pilgrim-way**